THE WEAPONS OF OUR WARFARE

ARE MIGHTY THROUGH GOD

By Nathaniel Richardson

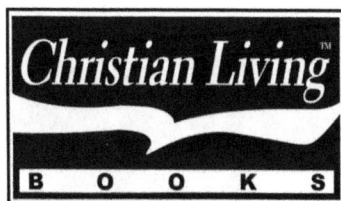

I0099122

Christian Living
B O O K S

Christian Living Books, Inc.
Largo, MD

ISBN 978-1-56229-368-0

Christian Living Books, Inc.
P. O. Box 7584
Largo, MD 20792
ChristianLivingBooks.com
We bring your dreams to fruition.

Unless otherwise marked, all Scripture quotations are taken from the King James Version of the Bible.

Printed in the United States of America

DEDICATION

I dedicate this book to my Father and His Son Jesus Christ my Savior for giving me the wisdom and knowledge to write this book.

To my wife, my children, and all my natural brothers and sisters. Thanks also to my father, mother, and all who helped me write this book.

CONTENTS

CONTENTS

BATTLEFIELD OF THE MIND

The battle against Satan is in the mind. It is there, in the faculty of consciousness and thought, that he places strongholds and evil imaginations to defeat us. He creates doubt, fear, feelings of unworthiness, confusion and brings those of us who are not cognizant of his strategies into captivity. Hence, the apostle Paul urges believers to offer our bodies as living sacrifices, holy and pleasing to God as a spiritual act of worship. He also admonishes us to renew our minds, which leads to the transformation of our lives. The renewal of our minds gives us better perspectives on life and changes our attitudes toward God, those around us, our circumstances, and ourselves. In the process, we discover God's pleasing and perfect will.

> *I beseech you therefore, brethren, by the mercies of God, that you present your bodies a living sacrifice, holy, acceptable to God, which is your reasonable service. And do not be conformed to this world, but be transformed by the renewing of your mind, that you*

> *may prove what is that good and acceptable and perfect*
> *will of God* (Romans 12:1-2).

Paul implores us to be made new in the attitude of our minds.
He encourages us to put on the new man created to be like God
in true righteousness and holiness. That is to say, we must all
put off falsehood and speak truthfully to everyone, for we are all
members of one body.

At times, evil spirits will taunt your mind. They will subtly try to
dissuade you from doing what you know you should. You will find
yourself saying, "I am not reading the Bible today. I am not praying today. Maybe tomorrow. I am not going to church this Sunday.
I am sick." Do not let these thoughts hold you down. Recognize
them as the enemy's tactics to set up strongholds in your life. Do
not entertain them; rather, you must pull them down.

Cast down every spirit that comes to your mind speaking evil,
creating arguments, and promoting high things that exalt themselves above the knowledge of God. Bring every thought into
captivity to obey Christ. Meditate day and night on God's Word
if you want to know what is written in it and if you want to
prosper.

Tormenting Spirit

I had an encounter some time ago with a little girl who was
about 16 or 17 years old. She was possessed with demons, and
her parents called me to come to their house to pray for her.
The devil had taken over her mind and was telling her to run
away. He tormented her so much she even attempted to hang
herself with a belt. This little girl did not say a word, but Satan
was talking through her telling me he was Lucifer.

Behold I give you authority to trample on serpents and scorpions and over all the power of the devil and nothing shall by any means hurt you (Luke 10:19).

We started to pray, and the devil tried to turn her head around to break her neck. She cried out loudly for about 30 minutes. I lay my hands on her and rebuked the devil. I commanded him to come out of her. Immediately, the demons came out and up to this day, she is still free from those spirits.

A certain centurion's servant who was dear to him got sick and was ready to die. Having heard about Jesus' power and authority, he sent elders of the Jews to ask Him to come and heal his servant. Jesus consented and started to walk to the centurion's house. However, on His way, the centurion sent friends to Him saying, "Lord, don't

> Jesus has authority over all evil spirits. They are servants under Him and also under us.

trouble yourself. I am not worthy that you should come to me. I did not even think myself worthy to come to you, but speak the word, and my servant will be healed."

The centurion spoke by faith. He continued by saying:

I also am a man placed under authority, having soldiers under me. And I say to one, 'Go,' and he goes; and to another, 'Come,' and he comes; and to my servant, 'Do this,' and he does it." When Jesus heard these things, He marveled at him, and turned around and said to the crowd that followed Him, "I say to you, I have not found such great faith, not even in Israel!" And those who were sent, returning to the house, found the servant well who had been sick (Luke 7:8-10).

Jesus has authority over all evil spirits. They are servants under Him; therefore, if we are saved and anointed by God, they are also under us. He has given us the authority to tell Satan, the devil, to come out of the people we are praying for. In the name of Jesus, he must obey.

> *The Spirit of the Lord is on me, because he has anointed me to proclaim good news to the poor. He has sent me to proclaim freedom for the prisoners and recovery of sight for the blind, to set the oppressed free* (Luke 4:18).

When I go to another city, country or state to preach, I pray and speak the Word of God. I command the evil spirits over that city, country or state to loose the minds of the people they are holding captive and set them free in the name of Jesus.

> *Verily I say unto you whatsoever ye shall bind on earth shall be bound in heaven: and whatsoever ye shall loose on earth shall be loosed in heaven* (Matthew 18:18).

The process of renewal comes when we read and study God's Word. Therefore, meditate on your Father's Word and watch Him change your life and the situations you face. Greater is He Who is in you than he who is in the world.

The devil tries to put evil thoughts in my mind, but I counter him by focusing on God's Word. A mind is a powerful thing to lose as a result of obeying the devil.

> *Trust in the LORD with all thine heart; and lean not unto thine own understanding. In all thy ways acknowledge him, and he shall direct thy paths* (Proverbs 3:5-6).

Prayer

Father, I agree in prayer with my brothers and sisters that every yoke be broken that I am talking about in this chapter. Every spirit must obey in the name of our Lord Jesus Christ. Amen.

2

GENERATIONAL
CURSES IN YOUR LIFE

*If they shall confess their iniquity, and the iniquity of
their fathers, with their trespass which they trespassed
against me, and that also they have walked contrary
unto me* (Leviticus 26:40).

Have you noticed patterns of dysfunctional behavior in your
life? Do you appear to be going through a sick cycle or have
strongholds that keep you in bondage? Many times, these repet-
itive behaviors that plague our parents, grandparents, and us are
generational curses. Such curses are not to be taken lightly. You
must take swift action to break the addictions, destructive hab-
its, depression or fear that bind you. If you do not acknowledge
these cycles as curses in your life, you cannot defeat them.

We often think of iniquity as an outward sin: lying, cheating, get-
ting drunk or sleeping around. However, iniquity in this context
refers to the perpetual, habitual sins of your forefathers. These
curses can extend as far back as your great-grandparents and
even beyond. Adultery, fornication, idolatry and so forth may
have been passed down the family line. If you want to be liber-
ated, you must take off the mask and admit you are facing these

challenges. There is not a person who has lived who does not struggle with or have some kind of issue plaguing his/her family. Instead of denying the problems, a better approach is to break the cycle so your children do not inherit the sick behavior you are battling with.

Refuse to see your children, father, mother, and other relatives messed up. Not only do you have an opportunity, but you also have a responsibility to establish a new pattern for your family. Unfortunately, many of us are afraid to face reality because we worry about what others might think about us. We fear their rejection. However, you don't need man's acceptance; you need God's deliverance. He will never reject you. In fact, you have already been accepted by Him. Is man's opinion more important than God's? The truth is it is likely that the very people you are hiding from have already seen the sickness oozing through anyway. Why hide it? It takes way too much energy trying to fake it and cover it up all the time. It is easy to look like the perfect, holy church man or woman who praises the Lord. Many people do it, even sinners praise God. However, does it make sense putting up a façade when you are living in private despair?

God loves you so much, He gave His only begotten Son that you can have everlasting, abundant life. Reject the generational curse. Cast down the evil imaginations that seek to destroy you and the lofty opinions that want to exalt themselves against the knowledge of God. Take every thought captive.

Learned Behavior

Much of what we do is learned behavior. We follow many of our forefathers' actions and behaviors. These practices then become strongholds that are supported by demonic influences.

Strongholds do two things. First, they keep people from knowledge and revelation truth. Secondly, they prevent people from walking in obedience. The lack of truth and rebellion cause you to perish.

> My people are destroyed for lack of knowledge (Hosea 4:6).

Strongholds are al so known as mindsets. A mindset is a fixed and rigid thought process that is resistant to change. The power of a spiritual stronghold is its ability to argue, reason or influence people to believe they cannot change. You absolutely *can* change with the power of God in your life. Nothing is impossible to

> Let go of the lies, criticism, guilt, and dysfunction. In their places, plant the truth.

us when we pray God's Word and break the generational curses over our lives. Give our Father the glory! When you have the authority of God and faith to remove mountains, you can cast down any generational curse.

How can I cast something down if I don't know it is contrary to the Word? What I know is that God's Word says I can live in perfect peace. I can refuse to let confusion rule my life. I will not stay up all night worrying, fretting, and having anxiety attacks over what might happen. The peace of God that passes understanding will keep my heart and mind by Jesus Christ (Philippians 4:7).

When this generational curse has been broken over your life, you must stay in the Word and pray. Give God the glory for setting you free. You are aware of the lies that have been passed down from your past, and you have rejected them. You must leave them behind and cleave to the Word of God. Let go of the lies, criticism, guilt, and dysfunction. In their places, plant the truth. Why is it important to occupy the spaces left by these vices? To stop them from returning with greater force.

When an unclean spirit goes through dry places seeking rest and finds none, it returns to the life from which it came. If that spirit finds it empty, it invites seven other spirits more wicked than itself to come along, and they re-enter the person. Sad to say, the last state of that man or woman is worse than it was originally. When God delivers you from evil spirits, you must fill your life with His Word. Secure your heart; do not follow this wicked generation that rejects Jesus and have fallen from the faith.

Therefore, my beloved brethren, be ye steadfast, unmovable, always abounding in the work of the Lord, forasmuch as ye know that your labour is not in vain in the Lord (1 Corinthians 15:58).

Prayer

Father, I pray that everyone reading book will understand the Word of God and that every generational curse be broken in their lives and the lives of their family members as well. In the name of Jesus Christ. Amen.

THE HOLINESS OF GOD

Happy is the man that findeth wisdom, and the man that getteth understanding. For the merchandise of it is better than the merchandise of silver, and the gain thereof than fine gold. She is more precious than rubies: and all the things thou canst desire are not to be compared unto her. Length of days is in her right hand; and in her left hand riches and honour. Her ways are ways of pleasantness, and all her paths are peace. She is a tree of life to them that lay hold upon her: and happy is every one that retaineth her (Proverbs 3:13-18).

And one cried unto another, and said, Holy, holy, holy, is the LORD of hosts: the whole earth is full of his glory (Isaiah 6:3).

I heard the voice of my Father saying, "Will you do my will?" I said, "Yes, Lord, here I am. Send me into the world to loose the chains of injustice, untie the cords of the yoke, share food with the hungry, and provide the poor wanderer with shelter. I will clothe the naked when I see them and not turn away from your own flesh."

If you make such a commitment to God, you will see light break forth like the dawn in your life. Your healing will quickly appear, and your righteousness will go before you. I say like Isaiah 6:3, "Holy, holy, holy Lord God Almighty." My Father is to be praised at all times because He is awesome. He is completely separate and absolutely free from sin and evil. He is totally good and pure. He is perfect light, perfect truth, perfect justice, and perfect love. Nothing can be fully compared to Him. No words can adequately describe Him. He cannot be explained, only exalted. He cannot be analyzed, only adored. He is not just holy but holy, holy, holy. What else can we say? His splendor is completely overpowering.

> *Do not come any closer, God said. Take off your sandals, for the place where you are standing is holy ground* (Exodus 3:5).

God our Father is awesome. He is exactly the same today as He was yesterday. He is not one degree less holy. His nature has not changed at all. He calls us to draw near. He calls us to be like Him. Looking back at the law, it immediately became clear that God's holiness is concrete. He is literally set apart and distinguished from this unclean and corrupt world. Hence, those who approach Him must also be separated from the things that defile. We must be separated, holy, and set apart for the service of God.

Under the Mosaic law, only unblemished offerings could be brought before God. After all, He is the holy God. Nothing else would be fitting; in fact, anything else would be insulting. There is a major lesson to be learned from this. We want a 100% restoration of the power and gifts of the Spirit; however, we only want to be 25% restored in morality, personal holiness, family life, and church structure. The doctrine we teach and the lifestyles we practice contradict each other. Therefore, we should not expect full restoration of the gifts; it simply will not happen that way.

> *Then Jesus said to his host, "When you give a luncheon or dinner, do not invite your friends, your brothers or sisters, your relatives, or your rich neighbors; if you do, they may invite you back and so you will be repaid. But when you give a banquet, invite the poor, the crippled, the lame, the blind, and you will be blessed. Although they cannot repay you, you will be repaid at the resurrection of the righteous"* (Luke 14:12-14).

> We are commissioned to make disciples of the nations and to win them before they are lost.

Although we are called by God to reach out to the poor and minister to the sick and afflicted, most of us have never prayerfully read Luke 14:12-14, let alone obeyed God by doing it.

Mercy and Grace

We are called to be one in the Lord and live united in our hearts and minds. However, each day, the church experiences new divisions. Even small congregations can experience a church split. We are commissioned to make disciples of the nations and to win them before they are lost, but we fail to do so. Some of our miserably shallow, shameless men deliver contradictory teachings. Of course, God does not demand perfection, and He does forgive; nevertheless, sin has ugly consequences. Our troubles will not just go away; there must be a judgment first.

Moses interceded for the Israelites after they refused to enter the Promised Land, and God responded by saying:

I have pardoned according to thy word: But as truly as I live, all the earth shall be filled with the glory of the LORD. Because all those men which have seen my glory, and my miracles, which I did in Egypt and in the wilderness, and have tempted me now these ten times, and have not hearkened to my voice; Surely they shall not see the land which I sware unto their fathers, neither shall any of them that provoked me see it: But my servant Caleb, because he had another spirit with him, and hath followed me fully, him will I bring into the land whereinto he went; and his seed shall possess it (Numbers 14:20-24).

Caleb had the right attitude toward God; he did not treat Him with contempt. Thus, the Lord rewarded him. We should approach the throne of God in humility to ask for mercy and grace, especially when it comes to the tragic lack of true holiness in our lives. Unfortunately, we have lost sight of the mark as obedient children. Scripture implores us not to give in to our evil desires. In everything we do, we are called to be holy as God is holy (1 Peter 1:14-16). That being said, it doesn't matter how serious the offense you have committed is, the Lord in Heaven will hear your prayer of repentance. He will honor a contrite heart.

The LORD is near to those who have a broken heart, and saves such as have a contrite spirit. Many are the afflictions of the righteous, but the LORD delivers him out of them all. He guards all his bones; not one of them is broken. Evil shall slay the wicked, and those who hate the righteous shall be condemned. The LORD redeems the soul of His servants, and none of those who trust in Him shall be condemned (Psalm 34:18-22).

Holy, holy, holy is our God, Father, and Lord Jesus Christ the Son of God. The High One says He lives forever. His name is holy. He lives in a high and holy place, but He is also with those who are lowly in spirit. He promises to restore His broken-hearted people. Those who are afflicted can rejoice because the Lord will not go back on His Word.

Glorify the Lord with me. Enter His holy place. Let us exalt His name together because He is awesome. I will praise the Lord. My soul and all that is within me will bless the Lord. I will bless His holy name.

I cannot forget all the love He gave me, for His love covers all my sins and yours too. He heals all of our diseases. God redeems us from the pit of hell and crowns us with love and compassion. He will satisfy your desires with good things so that your youth is renewed like the eagle's. The Lord made His ways known to the five-fold ministers who preach to the saints. The Lord works righteousness and justice for all the oppressed. Our Father is compassionate and gracious. He is slow to anger and abounds in love. He does not treat us as our sins deserve or repay us according to our iniquities. He will not always accuse, nor will He harbor His anger forever. For as high as the heavens are above the earth, so great is His love for those who fear Him (Psalm 103:1-11).

Holy, holy, holy is our Father who has compassion on His children. From everlasting to everlasting the Lord's love is with those who fear Him. It is with those who keep His covenant and remember to meditate and obey His Word.

The glory of God will come upon you when you are walking in true holiness. When my wife and I pray, the glory of the Lord shows up. One day, we were praying and speaking in tongues; we were drunk in the Spirit of the Lord. After that, I had to fight against a spirit of death that was trying to kill my wife's father. We spoke to that death spirit, rebuked it, and he left. Two days later, my wife got a call from her sister Julie. She told my wife that the doctor said if my father-in-law's nose had not stopped bleeding, he would have died. Of course, my wife and I knew that it was the power of God against the enemy that caused us to win the battle for her father's life.

If you are not saved, give God a try. He will bless you. God sent His Son Jesus into this world to die for you and me. His death facilitated the greatest miracle ever done on the earth: being born again. All the angels in Heaven shouted when you got saved, set free, and delivered. Give glory to God for your salvation!

> *That if you confess with your mouth the Lord Jesus Christ and believe in your heart that God has raised him from the dead, you will be saved* (Romans 10:9).

Prayer

> *Father, I ask that your people, who are called by Your name, will humble themselves and pray and seek Your face and turn from their wicked ways. I pray that they are strong in their minds and hearts. Let them be saved, set free, and delivered in the name of Jesus. Amen.*

4

I WENT TO HELL

And it came to pass, that the beggar died, and was carried by the angels into Abraham's bosom: the rich man also died, and was buried; And in hell he lift up his eyes, being in torments, and seeth Abraham afar off, and Lazarus in his bosom. And he cried and said, Father Abraham, have mercy on me, and send Lazarus, that he may dip the tip of his finger in water, and cool my tongue; for I am tormented in this flame (Luke 16:22-24).

The First Lady of a church in Chocowinity, North Carolina invited me to minister. She wanted me to preach on hell. I titled my message, "Hell Is for Real" based on Luke 16:19-31. In this passage, Jesus tells the story of a beggar whose name was Lazarus. He was covered with sores, which the dogs licked. He was so destitute that he ate whatever fell from the rich man's table. The time came when Lazarus died, and the angels carried him to Abraham's bosom. The rich man also died, but unlike Lazarus, he went to hell, a place of torment.

In hell, the rich man looked up and saw Abraham far away with Lazarus in his bosom. The tables had turned. Lazarus was comfortable and happy, but the rich man was miserable and tormented. Desperate, the rich man called out, "Father Abraham, have mercy on me. Send Lazarus to dip the tip of his finger in some water and cool my tongue, for I am tormented in this flame." However, Abraham replied, "Son, remember that in your lifetime you received the good things, but Lazarus got the bad ones. Besides all this, there is a great gulf fixed between us. So that those who want to pass from here to you cannot, and those from there cannot come to us."

My Visit to Hell

I was praying in my bedroom for about one hour and Jesus was standing on my left. He took me through a black hole for about five minutes and then we arrived in hell. I walked over to Satan, and immediately, he fell on his knees, lifted his hands and worshiped the Lord.

Jesus did not say anything while we were in hell. I was praying and speaking in tongues against Satan. He tried to be bold and stood to accuse me, but I was emboldened as well because I was not afraid of Satan. So I continued to speak in tongues with real power. I boldly declared as I had the right to, "For we wrestle not against flesh and blood but against principalities, powers, rulers of the darkness of this age, and spiritual wickedness in heavenly places." Once again, Satan fell on his knees with his hands lifted before the Lord. I continued to speak in tongues. The devil seeks to resist us, but once we pray, fast, and put on the armor of God, our faith will not fail.

In hell, I did not see Abraham and Lazarus in the "afar of" place the rich man was talking about. That place was no longer there. Why? Jesus went to the cross and died. He entered hell and took the keys from Satan. He preached to Abraham and the rest of the saints and carried them with Him to Heaven. He who was dead was raised on the third day by the power of God. He is alive forevermore. He swallowed up death and gave us the victory. Jesus died for all of us. Now, as He said, we have the keys of the kingdom of heaven, and whatever we loose on earth will be loosed in Heaven.

I was still praying in hell when someone called me as if he knew me. I turned to my left where Jesus was and said, "You messed up. You did not receive Jesus in your life when you had a chance, so you are here forever!" People were screaming and hollering, tormented in that fire. Jesus and I left hell and returned to my bedroom through the black hole.

> Once we pray, fast, and put on the armor of God, our faith will not fail.

The rich man in the scriptures told Abraham he had five brothers. He pleaded with Abraham to send Lazarus to his father's house to testify to them, so they would not end up in that place of torment.

Abraham made a profound statement to the rich man. He told him that if his brothers did not listen to Moses and the prophets, they would not be persuaded to change even if someone who rose from the dead begged them to. Well, I did not die, but I was taken to hell and came back to tell you to obey God's Word and be saved. You do not want to be in hell forever.

God said if the people of this world do not listen, they will be where the rich man is in hell. Therefore, those who have ears let them hear what the Spirit says to the people of the church and this world. Turn from your wicked ways and be saved before it is too late.

God told me to go into all the world and preach the resurrection of Jesus Christ to everyone. The people's wickedness is before Him. They are always learning but never know the truth, so they can be set free. They would not receive Jesus in their hearts.

Change your life because God loves you. In doing so, you will not be ashamed of the gospel of Jesus Christ, for it is the power of God that brings salvation to everyone who believes. Hell is real! I have been there, and I have come back to preach the gospel. Glory to God!

Prayer

Father, I pray that every reader be convinced to become saved and set free and that my beloved brother and sister be steadfast, unmovable, always abounding in the work of God. In Jesus' name. Amen.

CHAPTER

5

THERE IS POWER IN THE NAME OF JESUS

And when they were come to the multitude, there came to him a certain man, kneeling down to him, and saying, Lord, have mercy on my son: for he is lunatick, and sore vexed: for ofttimes he falleth into the fire, and oft into the water. And I brought him to thy disciples, and they could not cure him (Matthew 17:14-16).

A man brought his little boy to Jesus' disciples to be healed, but they could not do it. However, Jesus rebuked the demons causing the sickness, and they came out of the boy forthwith. Of course, the disciples wanted to know why they could not drive the demon out. Jesus explained it was because of their little faith.

Then Jesus answered and said, O faithless and perverse generation, how long shall I be with you? how long shall I suffer you? bring him hither to me. And Jesus rebuked the devil; and he departed out of him: and the child was cured from that very hour. Then came the disciples to Jesus apart, and said, Why could not we cast him out? And Jesus said unto them, Because of your unbelief:

27

for verily I say unto you, If ye have faith as a grain of mustard seed, ye shall say unto this mountain, Remove hence to yonder place; and it shall remove; and nothing shall be impossible unto you. Howbeit this kind goeth not out but by prayer and fasting (Matthew 17:17-21).

As Christians, we have to pray and fast, not only to cast out demons but so that people who enter our churches can be healed, set free, and delivered. They should never leave with the same problem they came in with except they want to. God can heal them by His power.

Nothing is impossible if you believe what God's Word says. You can speak to the mountains, and they have to move. The mountains spoken about here are spirits of the devil. When you say unto these spirits move from here to there, they will move in obedience to what God's Word says because He has given you the authority over the enemy. These spirits of the devil are servants unto us in the spirit. The only authority Satan has over us is what the Father gives to him. Faith in God's Word empowers us to do the impossible. Faith comes by hearing and hearing by the Word of God. Pray, fast, meditate on these scriptures, and watch the demons move out of your way.

Is not this the kind of fasting I have chosen: to loose the chains of injustice and untie the cords of the yoke, to set the oppressed free and break every yoke? (Isaiah 58:6).

Wiped Away

My wife had a vision that rain was falling on me but it could not soak me. It looked like when rain is falling on the front window of a car, and you wipe the water off with the windshield wipers. Likewise, the Spirit of the Lord moves the spirit of the devil off you.

I worked with a woman who practiced witchcraft. A man who could not hear or speak was in the room with her. I entered the room where they were, and she got angry with me for what seemed like nothing. However, I knew she was angry because the Spirit of the Lord entered the room. When the other person left the room, she was still talking. I turned around to walk out the door, but the Spirit of the Lord turned me around to confront

> If you have the faith to believe, you can remove mountains. Nothing will be impossible for you.

her. The Lord opened my mouth, and I said, "You do witchcraft around here on people. Hoodoo me if you *want* to."

I turned around, walked out the door and down the hallway wondering what in the world I had just said. However, I was not afraid. About 11:00 PM when I finished work, I went to my car. Seeds with blood stains were all over it. Nonetheless, I got in, drove home and prayed as I always do. I asked God to forgive her for what she did. The next day, I went to the job about 2:45 PM. When I entered the building, she was there. I looked her in the eye and said, "God bless you." Her mouth dropped open and her eyes got really big. She was *so* surprised that her witchcraft did not work on me.

> *Now to Him who is able to do exceedingly abundantly above all that we ask or think, according to the power that works in us* (Ephesians 3:20).

If you have the faith to believe what is said in this verse, you can remove mountains. That is why Jesus said nothing will be impossible for you. Therefore, as a child of God, you can confidently exercise your authority and command evil spirits (your servants) to come out of someone. As stated earlier, by faith, there is power in the name of Jesus. We are not talking about faith tomorrow or next year but faith *now*. You will have whatsoever you say. When Jesus cursed the fig tree because it did not have any fruit on it, the next day, the tree had dried up from the root. Peter was amazed at the sight.

> *For verily I say unto you, That whosoever shall say unto this mountain, Be thou removed, and be thou cast into the sea; and shall not doubt in his heart, but shall believe that those things which he saith shall come to pass; he shall have whatsoever he saith. Therefore I say unto you, What things soever ye desire, when ye pray, believe that ye receive them, and ye shall have them. And when ye stand praying, forgive, if ye have ought against any: that your Father also which is in heaven may forgive you your trespasses. But if ye do not forgive, neither will your Father which is in heaven forgive your trespasses* (Mark 11:23-26).

Before verses 23 and 24 of the preceding passage can work for you, you must obey verses 25 and 26. Faith without works is dead. Therefore, you must act on your faith and speak to those servants of yours, those evil spirits that torment the souls of people. Tell them to flee. Those demon servants must obey; it is written in my Father's Word.

Putting Marriages Back Together

One day, I was talking to my Father in prayer. He took me in the spirit to Pensacola, Florida to a married couples house. The devil was fighting their marriage. I descended from the sky and landed on the back porch. The dogs were barking at me, but they were tied up. I went into the house through the back door and spoke the Word over their marriage.

About 2 to 3 days after, I got a phone call from Val. She told me that her husband went into the living room and a big bright light was in the room. That was the Spirit of God and me in the room. After I rebuked the devil at their house, I went back home. They are still married today. Those spirits must obey you when you pray and fast before the Lord.

Now, I know why God permitted Satan to take me and my wife through marital problems and divorce. God said He was going to show me why He let me go through it, and He did. He uses me to put marriages back together, let the oppressed go free, and to break all yokes in marriages.

> As it is written: "For Your sake we are killed all day long; we are accounted as sheep for the slaughter." Yet in all these things we are more than conquerors through Him who loved us (Romans 8:36-37).

There is power in the name of Jesus Christ. By faith, Enoch was taken away; he did not see death (Genesis 5:24). By faith, Shadrach, Meshach, and Abednego were not burned in the fiery furnace. Three men went in but four were in the midst of the fire. The fourth one was like the Son of God. They came out unharmed and did not even smell like they were in the fire (Daniel 3).

It is impossible to please God without faith. No matter what it looks like or how bad it is, have faith in God that the mountains, which are demon spirits, will be cast out of your way. Call those things that do not exist as though they do exist. Do not be afraid.

God has not given you a spirit of fear but one of power in the name of Jesus Christ.

These Signs Follow

He said that in His name, you will drive out demons. You will lay your hands on the sick people, and they will be healed. These signs will accompany those who believe in the name of Jesus.

And these signs shall follow them that believe; In my name shall they cast out devils; they shall speak with new tongues (Mark 16:17).

I was preaching at a church in Nash County, North Carolina. After I finished preaching, a woman came up for prayer. The pastor had to communicate what she was saying because she had a stroke in the brain, so she could not speak. I rebuked the mountain that she had in her life, and it moved. She started talking. I gave God the praise because He is awesome in our lives.

Another woman in Grifton, North Carolina could not walk. After my wife and I prayed for her, she got up and walked. Praise the Lord! We will have what we say, and we will not live by bread alone. These are God's words. If my Father said I can remove mountains then I *can* remove mountains in His name.

If I do not doubt in my heart but believe that those things I say will come to pass, I will have whatever I say in the name of Jesus. I can do all things through Christ who strengthens me (Philippians 4:13). When I am weak in my understanding, it is then I am strong in the understanding of my Father's Word. We walk by faith, not by sight. Have you ever wondered why some prayers don't seem to be answered? Have you ever thought it is because you think God is angry with you? He is not mad at you. Walk in forgiveness each and every day and eliminate doubt from your heart. Doubt nullifies what faith desires to bring to pass.

By Faith

The key to answered prayers is having faith in God that your prayer requests will be answered. By faith, I did not die because of a brain aneurysm. By faith, my wife did not die because of the sickness of TTP-HUS. By faith, my daughter did not die because of double pneumonia. What are you asking God for? Do you want Him to save a family member, get you out of debt or draw you closer to Him? Do you believe He can give you your heart's desire? Do you truly believe He can do anything? If you believe it, you will have whatever you ask for. As you pray, have faith in God, not the problem. Have faith in God and not the circumstance. The enemy attacks all of us in our minds, homes, and finances. Are you feeling hurt and bruised because of the constant assault of the evil one? It is time to quench his fiery darts. It is time to walk in victory. It is time to take back what the devil has stolen from you. How? By picking up your shield of faith. Dust it off and use it daily, for the Word of God says it will quench all, not some but all the fiery darts of the wicked. The Spirit will help you overcome the enemy's attacks. If you are tired of being used and abused by the enemy, take your authority by faith and watch every attack, hindrance, stronghold, blockage, curse, and fiery dart put out.

> *And the apostles said to the Lord, "Increase our faith." So the Lord said, "If you have faith as a mustard seed, you can say to this mulberry tree, 'Be pulled up by the roots and be planted in the sea,' and it would obey you* (Luke 17:5-6).

As you cultivate faith in God in your heart, it will change the way you look at life. You will think and act differently. Spiritually, God surgically extracted those words from my personal vocabulary. How can you be a failure when God is still on His throne? How can you quit when you have the Word of God that cannot fail permeating your being? How can you be defeated when you have God's presence living inside of you? That is why I will have faith in what God said in His Word. He said I can lay hands on the sick and they will recover. I am the head and not the tail. I am above and not beneath. I will lend to many nations, but I will not borrow. He also said that by His stripes I am healed. He said He will make my ways prosperous and will have good success. I believe that too.

Forgetting those things which are behind and reaching forward to those things which are ahead, I press toward the goal for the prize of the upward call of God in Christ Jesus (Philippians 3:13-14).

God is speaking to you today. He knew you would need encouragement. He knew you would be looking for a word to direct, comfort, and deliver you. It is not by accident that you bought this book. God is specifically and clearly speaking to you. He wants you to know that He is able. I know you feel all alone sometimes, but He is always with you. I don't know what valley you are going through, what sickness is troubling you or what bills need to get paid this week. I don't know, but God does. He has a miracle scheduled for you with your name on it. Do not be afraid or dismayed, for the Lord your God is with you wherever you go. Have faith in Him, for He is able to turn your mess into a miracle, your confusion into comfort and your test into a testimony. He can wipe your tears away and put a smile on your face. Our Father has spoken; He is able to free you now.

Now faith is the substance of things hoped for, the evidence of thing not seen (Hebrews 11:1).

Grace and peace be unto you all from my Father and the Lord Jesus Christ.

Prayer

Father, I pray that each reader has the faith to be healed and set free from any problems in their life. I pray that they believe that by faith there is power in the name of Jesus Christ. Amen.

CHAPTER
6
BREAKTHROUGH COMING IN YOUR LIFE

When I wrote my first book, *Power Principles*, it took about three years before it got published. I was sitting down watching TV, and God told me to write the book. So, I did just that. My wife and I were praying about it for 3 years, and I almost forgot about it.

I got a call from my sister Bonnie. She introduced me to Kimberly the publisher who walked me through the process, step by step. After that, the devil was on my wife and me like white on rice. I did not know what was going on. It seemed as if we were in a boat, the bottom fell out, and we were sinking. I had to go to the emergency room twice, but they could find nothing. Bills were due. I did not have a job or any income. I did not know where the money would come from. I had to let Kimberly know what was happening. I texted her about it, and she was very understanding. She is an awesome woman of God who is anointed to do this work.

I thought about what God said in His Word about having faith in Him when I pray. One Wednesday at midnight, I reflected on Paul and Silas when they were praying at midnight and the earthquake took place. Inspired by that, I prayed and commanded the money to come to me forthwith. I had told Kimberly the money would be paid by Friday, and I don't like to go back on my word. By 5:00 PM the Thursday evening, the money came. The Lord had been working on my son Jeremy for about a week. When I prayed, he came and blessed me and my wife. He paid the bill off. Breakthrough came! I called Kimberly and told her about the payoff, and she said, "Look at God, Elder! I rejoice with you!" What an awesome God we serve.

You may be discouraged and fed up waiting in faith for your breakthrough. You say you have sown seeds but have not yet reaped, asked but have not yet received, sought but have not found. To everything there is a season and an appointed time. This is the season for your breakthrough.

When Jesus told Simon Peter to launch out into the deep and let down the nets for a catch, Simon Peter said, "Master, we have toiled all night long and caught nothing [obedience is better than worry]; nevertheless, at Your word, I will let down the net." When the disciples obeyed, they caught such a large number of fish that their nets began to break. They had to call their partners in the other boats to come and help them. Both boats were so full, they began to sink.

You will receive 100% more than you have. The harvest will be so great, you will not have enough room for it. Bless others with the overflow. You have been waiting a long time, but you are about to receive your breakthrough. Do not give up until you get your increase.

> *But those who wait on the Lord shall renew their strength; they shall mount up with wings like eagles. They shall run and not be weary. They shall walk and not faint* (Isaiah 40:31).

The Keys of the Kingdom

Think about the prophecies that were spoken to you and the dreams God gave you. Have faith in Him and watch Him change your situation. When Jesus said He would give us the keys of the kingdom of Heaven, He did so based on the authority of His Word. Jesus Christ released that authority to His church by shedding His blood on the cross. His sacrifice not only paid for our redemption but also vanquished Satan. By this act, Jesus led captivity captive and loosed the bondage of sin from all

> You are about to receive your breakthrough. Do not give up until you get your increase.

who will come to Him. Loosing in this context refers to the reason for our freedom and the redemption that has been accomplished through the blood of the Lord Jesus Christ.

We are also addressing a way of life. Being free and living free are two different things. Being free is a moment and certainly, an important one. It illustrates a person being unlocked from the chains in his/her life. However, living free is a life pattern. It is depicted by our standing up and walking in what His Word says about living free.

> *Stand fast therefore in the liberty by which Christ has made us free, and do not be entangled again with a yoke of bondage* (Galatians 5:1).

Repentance is more than simply saying, "I repent." The very word "repent" in the scriptures involves a stance of the mind, a reversal of attitude, a turning from one direction to another. However, it is a choice that can only be made in the light of God's truth, along with the understanding that it is patiently and graciously offered to people who need to repent and find the freedom Christ offers.

Can I Still Be Bound?

These two facts will, on occasion, puzzle some who will ask, "Are you saying that I may still be in bondage even though I've received Christ as my Savior? Can I still be trapped by the residue of my past experiences although I have been forgiven and made a new creature in Christ?" The answer is no. To say yes suggests that our salvation is incomplete. It is as if receiving Christ and being born again do not ready us for Heaven. The devil is a liar and the father of lies. Our salvation brings instant and complete justification through faith in Jesus Christ. The glorious reality is that we have not only been forgiven, but in the court where God alone is the judge of humankind, He has declared us not guilty. Court has been dismissed.

We are ready for Heaven. We have been completely received and regarded as saints after answering the call to grow in grace and in the knowledge of our Lord Jesus Christ. However, we are also called to holiness. If you examine God's Word from the beginning to the end, you will recognize that obedience is the key. You need to obey God's Word. When you disobey, the nightmares begin. You can't get your breakthrough if you resist. Do not live by bread alone but by every Word of God. Trust in what He says in His Word with all your heart and lean not on your own understanding. In all you do acknowledge Him, and He will direct your paths (Proverbs 3:5-6).

Simon Peter obeyed Jesus and reaped the rewards. He got his breakthrough by obeying Jesus' Word. Go back out there and drop your net. Get your breakthrough! Whatever God tells you to do, do it. Obedience is better than sacrifice.

> *For the weapons of our warfare are not carnal but mighty in God for pulling down strongholds, casting down arguments and every high thing that exalts itself against the knowledge of God, bringing every thought into captivity to the obedience of Christ* (2 Corinthians 10:4-5).

Don't Give Up

God reveals Himself in great ways when we obey His Word. Sometimes, you may feel like it's not going to work, but don't give up. Quitters never win. That's true in any arena of life. Your marriage isn't over until God says it is over. Hold on just a little while longer for your breakthrough. Hold on for your financial breakthrough. Don't be afraid to plant seeds even though your bills need to be paid. Plant a seed for your breakthrough. Whatever the circumstance, God has every resource you need. Fight the good fight of faith and win the challenge against the devil because the all-powerful, all knowing God lives within you. The sickness may be stronger than you, but it is not stronger than God.

God said His grace is sufficient for you. His strength is made perfect in your weakness. Therefore, when you are weak, it is then you are strong. It is not in your understanding but in His wisdom, knowledge, and understanding that you will overcome. Your enemies may think they are smarter than God in you, but they are not worthy enough to compare to the God in you.

> *Yet in all these things we are more than conquerors through Him who loved us. For I am persuaded that neither death nor life, nor angels nor*

41

principalities nor powers, nor things present nor things to come (Romans 8:37-38).

Nothing can stop your breakthrough. You will come out as a winner. God is about to bring you out triumphantly because He loves and cares for you and you obey His Word. To God be the glory!

Prayer

Father, I pray that the words You have given me to write in this book be a breakthrough for the readers and their families. I loose freedom in their lives in the name of Jesus Christ. Amen.

CHAPTER

7

THE NINE FRUIT OF THE SPIRIT

But the fruit of the Spirit is love, joy, peace, longsuffering, kindness, goodness, faithfulness, gentleness, self-control. Against such there is no law. And those who are Christ's have crucified the flesh with its passions and desires. If we live in the Spirit, let us also walk in the Spirit (Galatians 5:22-25).

Love

Love is a deep enduring concern for the welfare of others. It is affection and friendship. God's love is the ultimate example of pure, selfless love that is never-ending and all-encompassing. God's love for us is so great He chose to send His Son Jesus to die on the cross of Calvary to redeem us. Jesus chose to bear our sins and die on the cross to reconcile us to God. He commanded us to love one another as He loves us. In fact, there is no greater love than what Jesus demonstrated when He lay down His life for His friends; we are His friends. How should we respond when people do us wrong? Love and pray for them. It is by the fruit of love that people will know we are Christ's disciples. Every tree that does not bear good fruit is cut down and thrown into the fire.

> *And though I have the gift of prophecy, and understand all mysteries and all knowledge, and though I have all faith, so that I could remove mountains, but have not love, I am nothing* (1 Corinthians 13:2).

Above all, we must love each other deeply because love covers a multitude of sin. That's why Jesus died and on the third day by the power of God was resurrected from the dead.

Joy

Joy is gladness and rejoicing. It is not an emotion. Rather, it is a supernatural expression given to us by the indwelling of the Holy Spirit. Unlike happiness, which is a fleshly emotion that often depends on our circumstances, joy is a deep and abiding sense of contentment that provides a foundation for our lives in Christ. Joy grows and blossoms in the hard soil of tough times.

Psalm 30:5 says that weeping may endure for a night, but joy comes in the morning. The New Testament picks it up and says we do not have to wait until the battle is over; we can rejoice now (Philippians 4:4). Joy is one of the fruit of the Spirit living in us right now, for the joy of the Lord is our strength. Count it all joy when you fall into divers temptations. It will be difficult, but you can do it. You can do all things through Christ who strengthens you. You will never find joy by seeking self-centered excitement and pleasure. True joy comes when we give ourselves completely to God and yield to His will. True joy is the gift of knowing that our loving, heavenly Father holds our future in His hands. The joy of those who believe does not come from the world; therefore, the world cannot take it away.

Peace

Let the peace of God rule in your heart to which also you were called in one body, and be thankful (Colossians 3:15).

Peace I leave with you, My peace I give to you; not as the world gives do I give to you. Let not your heart be troubled, neither let it be afraid (John 14:27).

The peace of God is an inner calm we can experience only when we put in our all. In other words, we must put our future in His hands and fully trust Him for the results. When we face trials, we know He is in control. He has told us these things, so we may have His peace in this troubled world.

If you are born of God, you will overcome the world. Your faith gives you the victory to do so. You rest in His peace because your sins have been forgiven. You are right with God through Jesus Christ our Lord. Therefore, the peace of God, which passes all understanding will grant you favor in your heart and mind.

> You're born of God and will overcome the world. Your faith gives you the victory to do so.

The peace of God will keep you in your marriage, through your financial problems, and in all the devil throws at you. Peace kept me when the left side of my face was paralyzed, and I went to sleep with one eye open and the other eye closed. I did not see a doctor. In seven days, I was healed supernaturally.

Longsuffering

Longsuffering or patience is the ability to endure suffering, trouble or delay without being disturbed. Sometimes, it seems as if God does not care anything about what you are going through. It appears as though He does not love us. But He said He will never leave or forsake us. As born-again believers, when we face the difficulties of life, we must remember our faith is rooted in the belief that we will spend eternity walking on heaven's streets. Once we realize that everything we go through on earth is just for a little while, it should change our thinking. Blessed is the man who perseveres under trial because when he has stood the test, he will receive the crown of life that God has promised him (James 1:12). Clothe yourselves with compassion, kindness, humility, gentleness, and longsuffering.

> But let patience have its perfect work, that you may be perfect and complete, lacking nothing. If any of you lacks wisdom, let him ask of God, who gives to all liberally and without reproach, and it will be given to him (James 1:4-5).

You cannot have patience without the love of God. His is the kind of love that puts other people's needs above our own and does not seek personal gain. Most of the time, when I am facing severe challenges, I pray for other people's needs and forget my own. Let patience grow in you. Longsuffering is patience.

Gentleness

Gentleness is the quality or state of being kind. When we are told that we will bear the fruit of the Spirit called gentleness, what does that mean? Gentleness is directly tied to God's kindness. Because God is kind He is gentle. It is an attribute that flows directly out of God's disposition. We are saved by grace through faith because He is kind. It is not by anything we have done but by God's favor. Salvation produces God's fruit in your life. The way you look, your attitudes and actions will begin to change as you meditate on God's Word. The transformation will take place in your life as your mind is renewed. As your life changes, you will understand what is the good, acceptable, and perfect will of God.

Enabling others to succeed reveals kindness. Helping others achieve their goals is an act of kindness. You are growing in gentleness knowing that whatsoever good thing you do, you will receive from the Lord whether you are bond or free. If you show the fruit of gentleness today, it will re-enter your life in the future. This is the harvest of favor. One of the fruit of the Spirit that will grow in your life is kindness. It is the divine attribute that makes God's love come alive in us. It doesn't take away from God's goodness; rather, it makes God's goodness accessible to us.

Kindness is the patient love of God that caused His Son to humble Himself and leave the portals of Heaven to meet us where we are, so He could gently share His love with us. Showing God's kindness through your life is sharing the love and patience God bestowed upon mankind. It is not human nature to love others who are unloving toward you or to put the needs of others before your own. However, we can do so when the fruit of His Spirit is alive and working within our hearts.

Bearing with one another, and forgiving one another, if anyone has a complaint against another; even as Christ forgave you, so you also must do. But above all these things put on love, which is the bond of perfection. And let the peace of God rule in your hearts, to which also you were called in one body; and be thankful. Let the word of Christ dwell in you richly in all wisdom, teaching and admonishing one another in psalms and hymns and spiritual songs, singing with grace in your hearts to the Lord. And whatever you do in word or deed, do all in the name of the Lord Jesus, giving thanks to God the Father through Him (Colossians 3:13-17).

Goodness

It is easy to be good to those who are good to us, but as believers, we should also be good to those who have done us wrong. You will notice that love is incorporated in all the other fruit of the Spirit because it is the greatest fruit. Be full of the fruit of the Spirit, so you can admonish others to be good.

My wife and I have to be good to people. We have discovered that even if they are taking advantage of our kindness, God still produces fruit in our lives. God has given us all good things. One of the best ways to thank Him is by being good and loving to our brothers and sisters. If you refuse to do so, how can you be good and loving to God whom you have not seen? Goodness is defined as moral excellence, virtue, and excellence of quality. Goodness is not just appearing to be good; it is the essence of a person's character. However, we will never be good on our own as sinful human beings. The only way we can be good is by spending time with the source of all goodness – God.

God does not engage in evil activities. Seek to honor the Lord in your words, actions, and even your thoughts. Your life will overflow with thinking, doing, and being good through the encouragement of the Holy Spirit inside of you. Goodness will be seen in paying all your tithes and offerings. Plant seeds into the minister and watch God bring favor into your life because you have obeyed His Word.

Faithfulness

It is important to realize that God does not lose time because of preparation. Don't be anxious and jump ahead of Him. Promote God's Word, and He will promote you. You don't have to promote yourself. God will do that as you are faithful to do what He says. As you read and meditate on the Word, the Lord will reveal His will to you. After the disciples faithfully followed Jesus, they were promoted to apostles. Timothy and Titus traveled with Paul and were there to help him as he ministered to the churches. Then God promoted them to their own ministries. Philip the evangelist was called first to be a deacon. He waited tables faithfully before God exalted him to the ministry of an evangelist.

Sometimes, it will appear as if a minister is an instant success, but as you look closer, you will see that he was faithful to the things God called him to first, and then he was exalted. The Lord is looking for those who will commit to supporting ministries, so He can exalt them. They have proven themselves in the little things; hence, God can trust them with bigger things. Be faithful in whatever capacity you serve. If you are a supportive ministry assistant, associate deacon, giver, intercessor or secretary remember you are called and anointed by God to fill that position. You are vital to the success of that ministry. As you fulfill that role, God will exalt you.

Meekness

Those who are humble have the gentle, disciplined Spirit of God. Being meek does not mean you are weak. Actually, the Bible says the meek are blessed and will inherit the earth. They will delight themselves in the abundance of peace.

Scripture calls some wives to exercise meekness by submitting to their husbands. The merit in doing so is the influence our attitudes will have on the unsaved spouses. If they don't believe the Word, they will be won over when they see the purity and reverence in our lives. Your beauty should not come from outward adornments such as braiding your hair, wearing gold jewelry and fine clothes. Instead, your inner self should exude the unfading beauty of a gentle and quiet spirit, which is of great worth in God's sight. This is how the holy women of the past who put their hope in God used to make themselves beautiful. They were submissive to their own husbands.

In the same way, husbands ought to be considerate as they live with their wives. Treat them with respect as the weaker partner and as heirs with you of the gracious gift of life so that nothing will hinder your prayers.

Meekness is power under control. Meekness is like having the hands of a construction worker who labors on the highway all day; yet, when he gets home, he is able to gently hold a baby in his hands. That's the power of God's love in gentle action, and the fruit of gentleness alive in you. Be completely humble and gentle; be patient bearing with one another in love. To God be the glory.

Temperance

Self-control is having a level head and a sound mind.

> *His divine power has given to us all things that pertain to life and godliness, through the knowledge of Him who called us by glory and virtue, by which have been given to us exceedingly great and precious promises, that through these you may be partakers of the divine nature, having escaped the corruption that is in the world through lust. But also for this very reason, giving all diligence, add to your faith virtue, to virtue knowledge, to knowledge self-control, to self-control perseverance, to perseverance godliness, to godliness brotherly kindness, and to brotherly kindness love. For if these things are yours and abound, you will be neither barren nor unfruitful in the knowledge of our Lord Jesus Christ* (2 Peter 1:3-8).

As believers, we must exercise self-control and walk in God's will. Olympic athletes have an inner drive that motivates them to rise early in the morning to train. For Christians, that inner drive comes from the Holy Spirit. Self-control is the fruit of the Spirit that rises from within and calls us to live holy. Under God's control, we cannot be quick-tempered and greedy for money but hospitable, lovers of what is good, sober-minded, just, holy, and self-controlled.

> *Do you not know that those who run in a race all run, but one receives the prize? Run in such a way that you may obtain it. And everyone who competes for the prize is temperate in all things. Now they do it to obtain a perishable crown, but we for an imperishable crown.*

Therefore I run thus: not with uncertainty. Thus I fight: not as one who beats the air (1 Corinthians 9:24-25).

Prayer

Father, I pray that the Spirit moves in the readers. I pray that they get the understanding of the fruit of the spirit. I speak that the Holy Spirit set them free in the name of Jesus Christ. Amen.

INTERCESSORY PRAYER

Minister Jones, a powerful woman of God and a prayer warrior, was smelling a foul odor in her house. She asked her husband and son about the smell. They said they did not smell anything, but they were drowsy. The odor got stronger and stronger, and she knew something was not right. Time went by, and Minister Jones began to get lightheaded and weak. So, she asked her husband one more time. Again, he said he did not smell anything, so he went to bed.

Minister Jones knew in her spirit everything was not OK, but she had no idea what it was. I was praying on a Wednesday when the Holy Spirit nudged me to pray for Minister Jones. I told my wife, and we prayed in tongues. The following Friday, Minister Jones called the gas company to get someone to check out the smell. They came and told her the gas leak in her home was so bad, her house should have exploded in flames while they were sleeping. That's exactly what we were praying against. We asked God not to let the house explode. They fixed the gas leak. Intercessory prayer changes outcomes.

The Hebrew definition of "intercession" carries the concept of extending boundaries or territories by violence or by battle. In this case, intercession is translated *to fall upon*, as soldiers do in battle. Most times, warfare is required for the full extension of God's intended boundaries of blessing for people. The primary example of this usage is from a very negative circumstance in scripture:

> *Finally, my brethren, be strong in the Lord and in the power of His might. Put on the whole armor of God, that you may be able to stand against the wiles of the devil. For we do not wrestle against flesh and blood, but against principalities, against powers, against the rulers of the darkness of this age, against spiritual hosts of wickedness in the heavenly places. Therefore take up the whole armor of God, that you may be able to withstand in the evil day, and having done all, to stand. Stand therefore, having girded your waist with truth, having put on the breastplate of righteousness, and having shod your feet with the preparation of the gospel of peace; above all, taking the shield of faith with which you will be able to quench all the fiery darts of the wicked one. And take the helmet of salvation, and the sword of the Spirit, which is the word of God; praying always with all prayer and supplication in the Spirit, being watchful to this end with all perseverance and supplication for all the saints (Ephesians 6:10-18).*

Pray in the Spirit on all occasions with all kinds of prayers and requests. Be alert! Also, pray for your pastor that whenever he opens his mouth to preach the Holy Spirit will give him the words to say. That way, he will fearlessly make known the mystery of the gospel. Put on the complete armor of God when you are interceding in prayer. The Lord trained me how to pray in the Spirit. Every day, I would pray for about thirty minutes to an hour. During my prayer sessions, I learned how to pull down strongholds. Our weapons of warfare are not carnal but mighty through God. Therefore, we can all cancel the imaginations of the devil from our minds.

One day, I was praying for the pastor, and the Lord took me in the spirit to her house. Before I reached the house, I saw four angels. One was at every corner of the house standing up as a soldier. When I reached the house, I saw angels on each side of the bed where she was lying down. The angels were going back and forth leaning over her to minister to her. As you intercede for others in prayer, God will take you to see who you are praying for.

> Warfare is required to bring about the full extension of God's intended boundary of blessing.

A Watchman on the Wall

I was also praying for a woman from Haiti of whom I spoke in the first book I wrote. Her name was Mother Workman. She came from Haiti to speak at pastor Paul Thomas' church. That night, my wife and I visited the church. Right there, the Lord put Mother Workman on my heart. I had to hold her up in prayer. As time went by, I prayed and then I stop praying for her. When you are interceding for others, no matter what the circumstances, do not stop until what you are praying for is manifested.

Mother Workman returned to that same church to preach. I could not attend because I had to work, but my wife did. When Kate came home, she told me Mother Workman's testimony of the battle she was going through in the spirit realm. She was fighting against voodoo worshipers, and she was weak that night. I was troubled in my spirit with tears. That morning, when I got up, I prayed for her for about an hour. As I was praying, my Father took me in the spirit to Haiti. I was on the top of Mother Workman's house. I saw a man lying down at the foot of her bed, and the evil spirit saw me looking down at him. The man jumped, so I rebuked the unclean spirit and returned home. The next night, Mother Workman testified that three hundred voodoo worshipers got saved. That was her victory in the Lord Jesus Christ.

> *Likewise, the Spirit also helps in our weaknesses. For we do not know what we should pray for as we ought, but the Spirit Himself makes intercession for us with groanings which cannot be uttered. Now He who searches the hearts knows what the mind of the Spirit is, because He makes intercession for the saints according to the will of God* (Romans 8:26-27).

> *Bless the Lord, O my soul: and all that is within me, bless his holy name* (Psalm 103:1).

Prayer

> *Father, I pray that my brothers and sisters are praying always with all prayer and supplication in the spirit being watchful to this end with all perseverance and supplication for all saints in the name of Jesus Christ. Amen.*

9

THE NINE GIFTS OF THE SPIRIT

There are diversities of gifts, but the same Spirit. There are differences of ministries, but the same Lord. And there are diversities of activities, but it is the same God who works all in all. But the manifestation of the Spirit is given to each one for the profit of all: for to one is given the word of wisdom through the Spirit, to another the word of knowledge through the same Spirit, to another faith by the same Spirit, to another gifts of healings by the same Spirit, to another the working of miracles, to another prophecy, to another discerning of spirits, to another different kinds of tongues, to another the interpretation of tongues (1 Corinthians 12:4-10).

Wisdom

Wisdom can be defined as understanding and knowledge gained by experience. God has all wisdom and all knowledge. He knows everything; however, He never reveals everything He knows to anybody. He just reveals some of what He knows. A word is a fragmentary part of a sentence, and so it is with wisdom. God does not reveal the gift of wisdom but the word of wisdom to a man. He only gives him the part He wants him to know. For example, if you needed legal advice, you would call a lawyer, but the lawyer wouldn't give you all the legal wisdom he has because you wouldn't need all of it. He would just give you a word of the wisdom that fits your particular case. He gives you a word of wisdom, legal wisdom, and that is really all you need. The word of knowledge is a supernatural revelation by the Spirit of God concerning certain facts in the mind and will of God.

The difference between these two gifts, the word of knowledge and the word of wisdom is that the revelation, which the word of knowledge brings, is always present knowledge. Alternatively, it is the knowledge of something that happened in the past. On the other hand, the word of wisdom speaks about the future.

The word of wisdom and the word of knowledge often operate together. For example, when you are at the church and your pastor has finished preaching, the Spirit will move, and the five-fold ministries will begin to function. It is possible you may be called out and given a word of wisdom.

Knowledge

Sometimes the word of knowledge comes in a word of revelation. Jesus did this with the woman at the well in Samaria. He used the word of knowledge to convince her, a sinner, that she needed a Savior. This woman asked Jesus who He was, and He answered, "If you knew who I was you would not have asked me. I will give you water, so you will never thirst again."

She said, "Give me this water, so I won't have to come here and draw water again."

Jesus said, "The water I give you will be in you a well of water springing up into everlasting life." The woman wanted that water.

Jesus told her to go and get her husband. However, she told Him she had no husband. He told her she was right about that because she had five husbands, and the man she was living with at the time was not her husband. Jesus knew this by an inward revelation, a word of knowledge. He used this gift to point her to salvation. The word of knowledge can be manifested in a number of different ways. It may come through tongues and interpretation through the gift of prophecy, or an angel may come to deliver a word of knowledge. God has many ways of doing things. Often, these gifts operate together; we just separate them in order to define them. Sometimes the gift of the word of knowledge is confused with a profound knowledge of the Bible. God helps us to understand His Word, and we receive knowledge from studying it; that kind of knowledge is not a supernatural gift.

> God has many ways of doing things. Often, the nine gifts operate together.

The word of knowledge does work in connection with the Bible. God reveals things in connection with His Word, which we do not know. But if that were all there were to it, we wouldn't have to study. Paul told Timothy the young pastor of a New Testament church to study. Paul said, "Study to show thyself approved" (2 Timothy 2:15). So, this particular kind of knowledge of God's Word comes by studying. But the word of knowledge comes by supernatural revelation imparted by God.

The Spirit moved in to save Odie and Val Jackson's marriage from breaking up as mentioned earlier. Thank God for the word of knowledge in the time of need. It can be distributed to each individual as God wills.

Faith

The gift of faith is not imparted to all. It is only given as the Spirit wills. Also, it is a supernatural manifestation of the Holy Spirit to receive a miracle. A person does not perform a miracle by the gift of faith, but he passively receives a miracle by that gift. The gift of faith is distinguished from the other kinds of faith in that with this special faith, there is a manifestation of the evidence of the supernatural. One can supernaturally, and against all odds, believe God for a miracle. Of the three powerful gifts: the gift of faith, the working of miracles, and the gift of healing, the gift of faith is the greatest.

There are three different kinds of faith: general faith, the gift of faith, and saving faith. General faith gives a supernatural ability to receive a miracle from God. It could be for supernatural protection, supernatural sustenance, the raising of the dead or the impartation of supernatural manifestations such as in the laying on of hands for receiving the Holy Spirit. On occasion, the gift of faith may be used to cast out unclean spirits from people whose bodies have been defiled by them. Here again, more than one gift must be in operation.

The gift of discerning of spirits and or the word of knowledge will be manifested, as well as the gift of faith. If one doesn't discern or see the spirit, often the spirit is revealed through the word of knowledge. But the gift of faith must still be exercised to cast out the spirit. Of course, we know from Mark 16:17 that general faith is also effective in casting out evil spirits. I had to cast unclean spirits out of a man who was a witchcraft worshiper. You can read about that in my first book, *Power Principles.*

Healing

Healing can be defined as the restoration of health. Healing, like the other gifts, is a supernatural manifestation of the gift of God. We may have some difficulty because of our limited knowledge in defining some of the other gifts. However, there should be little difficulty in defining the gift of healing. Nearly everyone understands healing. Of course, Jesus brought healing into prominence by His ministry. He also gave authority to His disciples to heal the sick.

Heal the sick, cleanse the lepers, raise the dead, cast out demons. Freely you have received, freely give (Matthew 10:8).

We want to emphasize the supernatural character of all the gifts of the Spirit including the gift of healing. These gifts have nothing to do with medical science or human learning. God heals a lot of people in the hospitals. Don't get me wrong. God can heal in the hospital, too. That's what doctors are here for – to work on you as God works on healing you. But the gift of healing, a supernatural manifestation comes straight from God. Luke the beloved physician was with Paul on his missionary journeys. Luke wrote the book of Acts of the Apostles, as well as the Gospel that bears his name.

He was with Paul when he was shipwrecked on the island of Malta (Acts 28); yet, nothing is said to the effect that Luke ministered to the people with his medical knowledge. In fact, Luke records that the father of the chief man of the island was sick and Paul laid his hands on the man, and he was healed by the supernatural power of God. Then the people brought those who were sick on the island for Paul to minister to them, and they were healed. The purpose of the gift of healing is to deliver the sick and destroy the works of the devil in the human body.

> *And His disciples asked Him, saying, "Rabbi, who sinned, this man or his parents, that he was born blind?" Jesus answered, "Neither this man nor his parents sinned, but that the works of God should be revealed in him* (John 9:2-3).

Many people are born into this world with no legs, blind, deaf, lame, and all kinds of sicknesses. Healing can be a supernatural manifestation in our lives so that God can be glorified. This gift worked on me a number of times. As said earlier, the left side of my face was paralyzed for 7 days, and I did not go to the doctor. God healed me. Well, it returned for 14 days, and you know what? My Father did it again. He is an awesome Father.

Miracles

Miracles are sometimes translated as signs, wonders or mighty acts. The working of miracles in manifestation is seen when Jesus took a little boy's lunch, fed the five thousand with it and then gathered up twelve baskets of leftover food after the people had eaten. The working of miracles was also used to confirm the Word that was preached. When Paul was preaching in Cyprus, Elymas the sorcerer withstood him. Paul, through the power of God in the operation of the gift of working of miracles, struck him blind for a season; that was a sign to others. This gift was also used to deliver people from unavoidable danger.

The gift of faith will carry a person through danger without being harmed at all; however, the working of miracles is different. It will actually change the circumstances causing the danger. When Jesus stood in that ship during a storm on the Sea of Galilee and said, "Peace be still," that worked a miracle, which changed the very circumstances causing the danger. The difference between the gift of faith and the working of miracles is that the gift of faith receives a miracle and the working of miracles works a miracle.

> *Behold, I will bring the shadow on the sundial, which has gone down with the sun on the sundial of Ahaz, ten degrees backward." So the sun returned ten degrees on the dial by which it had gone down. This is the writing of Hezekiah king of Judah, when he had been sick and had recovered from his sickness* (Isaiah 38:8-9).

One day, my brother Burlee and I were trying to get on the bus. It started to rain, but I commanded the rain to stop, and it did. A miracle is a supernatural event occurring in the ordinary course of nature. God temporarily suspended the rain and a miracle was manifested that day.

Prophecy

Prophecy is speaking for God. The simple gift of prophecy should not be confused with the prophecy office.

> *He that prophesieth speak unto men to edification and exhortation and comfort* (1 Corinthians 14:3).

Thus, we can readily see that in the simple gift of prophecy, there is no revelation. In the office of a prophet, however, we often find revelation coming forth even by prophecy.

It is also interesting to know the difference between prophecy in the Old and New Testament. In the Old Testament, prophecy is essentially foretelling future events; whereas, in the New Testament, it shifts strongly to foretelling the simple gift of the prophet. There is no foretelling of the future whatsoever. Notice that Paul is telling the entire church at Corinth to prophesy and to desire spiritual gifts; however, he preferred if they prophesied. Yet, Paul had just gotten through telling them in Chapter 12 of 1 Corinthians that God has set in the church "first apostles, secondarily prophets, thirdly teachers" (1 Corinthians 12:28).

Paul goes on to ask, "Are all apostles?" The answer is no. "Are all prophets?" No, they couldn't be. If prophesying makes you a prophet, then Paul would be contradicting himself. Evidently, the fact that you have prophesied doesn't make you a prophet. It means you have exercised the simple gift of prophecy. For example, a rich man has money. In fact, all of us have some money, but that doesn't make us rich. By the same token, a prophet prophesies, but everyone who prophesies is not necessarily a prophet. A prophet, for example, would have more of the gift of the Spirit in operation than just the gift of prophecy. He would have revelation gifts operating along with prophecy.

Paul said in 1 Corinthians 14:29, "Let two or three prophets speak and let the others judge." Then in verse 30, he said, "If anything be revealed to another that sitteth by (that is another prophet), let the first hold his peace. For you can all prophesy one by one, that all may learn and all may be encouraged." To stand in the office of the prophet, a person must have the gift of prophecy operating in his ministry, plus, at least, two of the revelation gifts: the word of wisdom or the word of knowledge and the gift of discerning of spirits.

I am an ordained prophet and minister. A true prophet says exactly what God's Word says. Both men and women serve as prophets.

Discerning of Spirits

Discerning of spirits is the ability to tell whether someone is speaking by the Holy Spirit or a false spirit. The nine gifts of the Spirit can be divided into three categories: three gifts that reveal something, three gifts that do something, and three gifts that say something. The three gifts that reveal something are the word of wisdom, the word of knowledge, and the discerning of spirits.

The three power gifts (as they are often called) that do something are the gift of faith, the working of miracles, and the gift of healing. The three inspiration gifts are prophecy, divers kinds of tongues and the interpretation of tongues. Often, these gifts work together as in the case of tongues and interpretation. However, we divided them here to distinguish and study them. Our previous lesson dealt with two of the three gifts, which reveal something: the word of wisdom and the word of knowledge. In this lesson, we will cover the third revelation gift: the discerning of spirits. The most important of the three revelation gifts, of course, is the word of wisdom. Listed in the order of their importance they realer are. The word of wisdom gives us a revelation of the mind and purpose of God; anything else deals with the future.

As mentioned earlier, the word of knowledge gives us a revelation of things in the present or past. The discerning of spirits gives us insight into the spirit world. It actually has a more limited range than the other two revelation gifts because its revelation is limited to a single class of spirits. The revelation that the word of wisdom and the word of knowledge brings is broader and applies to people and things; whereas, the discerning of spirits gives supernatural insight into only the realm of spirits. Let me say that the discerning of spirits has to do only with the realm of the spirit—both good and bad. The discerning of evil spirits is included, but too many people have thought the discerning of evil spirits is all this gift refers to. However, it also refers to good spirits.

> *Beloved, do not believe every spirit, but test the spirits, whether they are of God; because many false prophets have gone out into the world. By this you know the Spirit of God: Every spirit that confesses that Jesus Christ has come in the flesh is of God, and every spirit that does not confess that Jesus Christ has come in the flesh is not of God. And this is the spirit of the Antichrist, which you have heard was coming, and is now already in the world* (1 John 4:1-3).

All thanks to our Father and His Son Jesus Christ.

Different Kinds of Tongues

The word "divers" is in the King James Version, which means it was added by the translator. Actually, the verse reads "another kind of tongues." Later, in the same chapter, Paul said that God set in the church diversities of tongues. Therefore, it would be acceptable to say that "divers kinds of tongues" is the supernatural utterance by the Holy Spirit in languages never learned by the speaker, not understood by the mind of the speaker or necessarily understood by the hearer. Speaking with tongues has nothing whatsoever to do with linguistic ability. It has nothing to do with the mind or the intellect of man. It is a vocal miracle! The gift of tongues is the most prominent of the three vocal gifts or as they are sometimes called, gifts of utterance or inspiration: the gift of prophecy, divers kinds of tongues, and the interpretation of tongues.

This doesn't necessarily mean the gift of tongues is the best, but it is the most prominent for several reasons. Discussing public ministry in tongues, Paul said, "If any man speak in an unknown tongue, let it be by two or, at the most, by three." Of course, one person would interpret. If there is no interpreter, the person should keep silent in the church and speak to himself and God.

> If anyone speaks in a tongue, let there be two or at the most three, each in turn, and let one interpret. But if there is no interpreter, let him keep silent in church, and let him speak to himself and to God (1 Corinthians 14:27-28).

In Greek, the words "two" and "three" are personal pronouns and refer to people. Paul was saying not more than two or three people should speak in a church service. In the next verse, he said to let the prophets present who could speak. We need to be very careful to walk softly before the Lord. We should remain open to Him as we deal with spiritual matters quietly, honorably, reverently, and invite the operation of the Spirit of God among us.

Interpretation of Tongues

The interpretation of tongues is the supernatural revelation by the Spirit of the meaning of an utterance in tongues; it is the interpretation of tongues. The gift of interpretation is the last of the nine gifts of the Holy Spirit because it is dependent upon another gift to operate. It does not function unless the gift of tongues is present. It makes tongues intelligible to hearers so that the church, as well as the possessor of the gift, may know what has been said and may be edified.

> *I wish you all spoke with tongues, but even more that you prophesied; for he who prophesies is greater than he who speaks with tongues, unless indeed he interprets, that the church may receive edification* (1 Corinthians 14:5).

Greater is he who prophesies than he who speaks with tongues, except he can interpret that the church may receive edification. But can God speak to us in some other way? Yes, He can and does. We have messages which are not an interpretation of tongues, they are a manifestation of the gift of prophecy. All these gifts operate by faith, but it takes more faith to prophesy than to give an utterance in tongues or interpretation of tongues. This is so because those who operate in these gifts have to lean on others. In other words, the person with the gift of tongues can lean on the one with the gift of the interpretation of tongues. However, the person who has the gift of prophecy must have enough faith just to start speaking what he has received.

> *And they were all filled with the Holy Spirit and began to speak with other tongues, as the Spirit gave them utterance* (Acts 2:4).

> *He who speaks in a tongue edifies himself, but he who prophesies edifies the church* (1 Corinthians 14:4).

May grace and peace be with you all from my Father and His Son Jesus Christ. Hallelujah!

Prayer

> *Father, I pray that with the nine gifts of the Spirit the church will tear down the kingdom of the devil because He has anointed us to preach the gospel to the poor. He has sent us to heal the brokenhearted and to proclaim liberty to the captives and recovery of sight to the blind and to set at liberty those who are oppressed in Jesus' name. Amen.*

10

GOD IS ABLE

God is able. He has brought me out of so much I cannot tell it all. He can bring you out of what you are in also. He is well aware you will need encouragement to believe Him. He said He will never leave you or forsake you. It is important to Him that you understand His ability to handle the issues you face in life. Take your mind off everything else and put it on God because He can help you.

I know sometimes we feel like God is not there and if He is, He simply doesn't care. But He does. He is always with you, even in the difficult seasons of your life. I don't know what problem you have, what dilemmas you are going through, what sickness is troubling you or what bill you need to pay today. Whatever it is, I assure you that God is able. No matter what the devil says or how severe the pain is, God is able. I don't know what your life looks like, but God is able. He has a miracle scheduled for you with your name on it.

Look, the Lord your God has set the land before you; go up and possess it, as the Lord God of your fathers has spoken to you; do not fear or be discouraged (Deuteronomy 1:21).

On July 31, 2000, the devil tried to take my life, but God said no. The doctor said I had TTP-HUS, which is a disorder that causes the red blood cells to eat up the white blood cells. He said I was not going to make it. But God is able. I am here today to tell you that God will bring you out and set you free from whatever you are in. Trust Him to turn your mess into a miracle, your confusion into comfort, and your test into a testimony. Hold on to God. Don't let go because He will bring you out.

Many Christians go through life bound because they do not believe God is able. Christ did it all for you. Do not let the devil fill your mind with dirt, lies or half-truths that God cannot help you. All you need to do is speak God's Word. My daughter Tameka had pneumonia when she was 8 months old. She was very sick. I took her to the hospital and the doctor said I got there just in time. If I had not gotten there when I did, she would have died. She was hospitalized for three days and three nights. The devil did not win. He thought he did, but God performed a miracle.

Now to him who is able to do exceedingly abundantly above all that we ask or think according to the power that works in us (Ephesians 3:20).

Prayer

My Father, I pray concerning this book You inspired my wife and I to write. We know the weapons of our warfare are not carnal but mighty in God. They pull down strongholds and cast down imaginations and every high thing that exalts itself against the knowledge of God. They also bring into captivity every thought to the obedience of Christ. Father, set all those who read this book free from the crown of their heads to the soles of their feet. Let them know whatever they are going through You can fix it. In the name of Jesus Christ. Amen and amen.

ABOUT THE AUTHOR

Nathaniel Richardson is a native of Vredenburgh, Alabama. He has been an ordained minister for over thirty-five years. An Elder and Prophet at Redeeming Faith Ministries International, he is active in ministering to the lost and broken and preaching the gospel of the Kingdom. He and his wife, Wanda, have five children and reside in Greenville, North Carolina.

www.ingramcontent.com/pod-product-compliance
Lightning Source LLC
Chambersburg PA
CBHW062027040426
42447CB00010B/2166